CHRISTMAS
ACTIVITY BOOK

By Catherine Bruzzone

Illustrated by Clare Beaton

BARRON'S

Christmas Fun

On the following pages you'll find lots of ideas for things to make to brighten up your Christmas.

And you can take a break from all that busy activity to enjoy these games and puzzles:

On page 24, you will find out how people celebrate Christmas around the world.

And don't forget to make up the mouth watering Advent Calendar in the center of the book.

This Christmas robin will be hopping through the book with you.
See if you can spot him on each page.

What You Need

★ Always be careful with sharp tools such as scissors, staplers, and needles.
★ For some of the activities you'll need to use a craft knife. This symbol will remind you to be extra careful.

Some basic tools and materials:

paint
glue
scissors
paper (different colors)
cardboard (different colors)
crayons
colored pencils
felt-tip pens
stapler
hole puncher

Very useful:

tissue paper
crêpe paper
colored felt
glitter
tinsel
aluminum foil
stickers
face paints

You don't have to buy everything.
Start a "Christmas collection" to save:
  cards
  wrapping paper (especially silver
    and gold)
  scraps of material
  chocolate and candy wrappers
  yarn
  ribbon

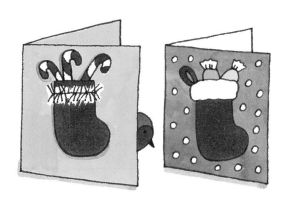

Stocking collage

What you will need

★ card
★ scissors
★ glue
★ scrap of red felt
★ aluminum foil or silver candy wrappers
★ thin ribbon or paper ribbon
★ glitter
★ felt-tip pen (for message)
★ candies or small gifts

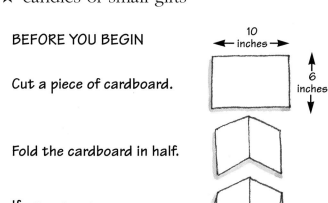

BEFORE YOU BEGIN

Cut a piece of cardboard.

Fold the cardboard in half.

If you use paper,
fold it into quarters.

1

Take a piece of red felt. Cut out the shape of a thick stocking.

2

Leave space above stocking.

Don't glue here.

Glue the edge of the stocking. Stick it on the card. Leave the top open.

3

Write message inside.

Fill with candy.

Dab glue and

around card.

sprinkle glitter

Cut a strip of aluminum foil and tie a ribbon. Glue them along the top of the stocking.

Star stencil

Once you have made your stencil, you can print several of these cards.

What you will need

★ newspaper (for protection)
★ dark colored paper (for card)
★ thick cardboard (for stencil)
★ craft knife or sharp scissors—be careful!
★ white or yellow poster paint
★ sponge or paintbrush
★ glue
★ glitter
★ felt-tip pen (for message)

BEFORE YOU BEGIN
Cover a table or the floor with newspaper. Put on an apron or overalls.

1

Use star template if you can. star shape doesn't have to be perfect.

Make a stencil. Draw a star on thick cardboard and cut around it.

2

You could splatter paint with a brush.

Put the stencil over the front of the cardboard. Sponge on the paint.

3

Write message inside.

Dab glue around the edge of the star. Sprinkle glitter onto the glue.

Here are three ways of making pretty gift tags.

What you will need

★ old Christmas cards
★ scissors
★ hole puncher
★ pieces of cardboard
★ stickers
★ glitter
★ felt-tip pen (for message)
★ for potato prints, see page 14

1

Cut different shapes.

Cut up old Christmas cards. Choose parts with no writing on the back.

to Grandma Merry Christmas love Ka XXX

Use a hole puncher to punch a hole. Thread yarn through the hole.

2

Cut small rectangles from cardboard. Make a pattern with stickers.

3

Add glitter.

Cut small rectangles of cardboard. Print shapes with potato cuttings. (See pages 14 and 15.)

Santa's Trail

Can you spot ten differences between these two pictures?

Two paper chains

What you will need

★ different wrapping paper
★ 2 rolls of different colored crêpe paper
★ scissors
★ glue or double-sided tape

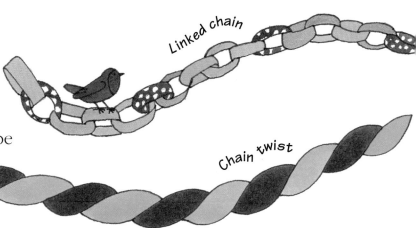

Linked chain

Chain twist

1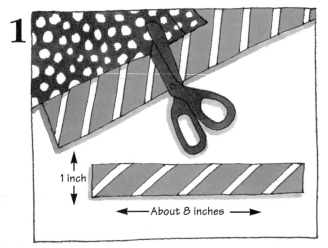

1 inch

← About 8 inches →

Cut strips of different wrapping paper.

2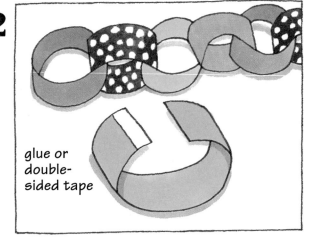

glue or double-sided tape

Glue each strip together to link the chain.

1

1 inch wide

Cut a strip from the end of 2 rolls of different colored crêpe paper.

2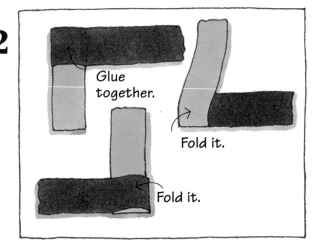

Glue together.

Fold it.

Fold it.

Glue the ends together. Fold one strip over the other. Glue the end. Stretch it.

Cut a rectangle of black paper. Draw a frame and bell shape in chalk.

Stained glass window

What you will need

★ thick black paper
★ chalk or white crayon
★ craft knife or sharp scissors—be careful!
★ colored tissue paper
★ glue or tape
★ string

2

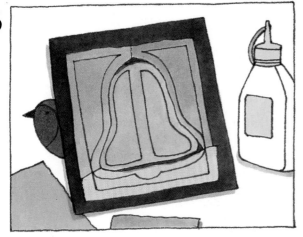

Cut out the bell shape. Make sure it touches the frame on 3 sides.

3

Glue or tape pieces of tissue paper to the back. Use different colors.

string

hole

Hang it in your bedroom window.

Lanterns

What you will need

★ old wrapping paper, colored paper, or colored foil
★ pencil
★ ruler
★ scissors
★ glue

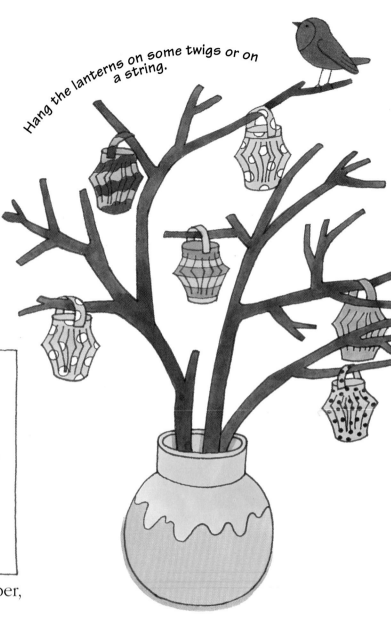

Hang the lanterns on some twigs or on a string.

1

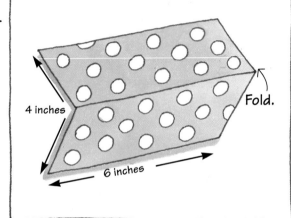

4 inches

6 inches

Fold.

Cut a rectangle from wrapping paper, colored paper, or aluminum foil.

2

Leave ½ inch

Fold it in half. Cut narrow strips along the fold. Don't cut to the edge.

3

Glue on paper strip for handle.

Glue.

Spread the paper open. Curve it around and glue the edges together.

Tricky Trees

Each of these Christmas trees has one thing missing.
Can you see what it is?

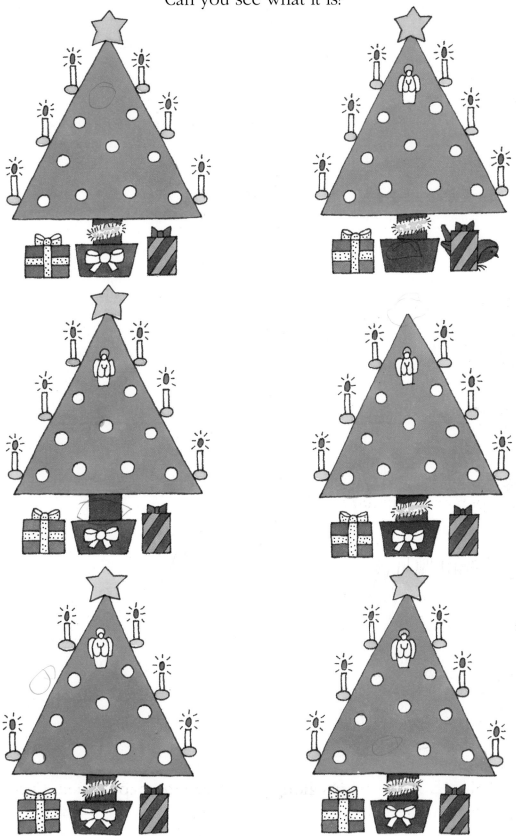

Journey to Bethlehem

This is a game for 2–3 players.
You will need 3 markers and a die.
Mary and Joseph, the three kings, and the shepherds are all traveling to Bethlehem. Which group will arrive first? Pick a group. The youngest can start, then the player on his or her right. Throw the die to move along the board. The winner is the first to the stable.
Do you know who reached the stable first in the real nativity story?
Do you know why Mary and Joseph were traveling to Bethlehem?

Donkey still fresh.
Go forward 4.

Lose lamb.
Miss a turn.

Path goes downhill.
Go forward 6.

Mary too stiff to ride.
Miss a turn.

Take short cut.
Go forward 3.

Joseph offered lift in cart.
Go forward 3.

Excited by angel's words.
Go forward 4.

Stop for rest.
Miss a turn.

Carry smallest lamb.
Go forward 2.

12

Shepherds

Joseph

3 Kings

Star shines brightly.
Go forward 4.

...ough valley.
...d 6.

Well-trodden track.
Go forward 6.

Stuck in sand dune.
Miss a turn.

Don't stop for rest.
Go forward 3.

Leave frankincense at picnic spot.
Go back 2.

Fresh water at oasis.
Go forward 2.

Camel lame.
Miss a turn.

Get lost in mountains.
Go back 2.

See Bethlehem in distance.
Go forward 2.

Mary too tired to travel.
Miss a turn.

Cloudy night, no star.
Go back 1.

NO ROOM

No room at inn.
Go back 1.

...g road.

Can't find stable.
Go back 1.

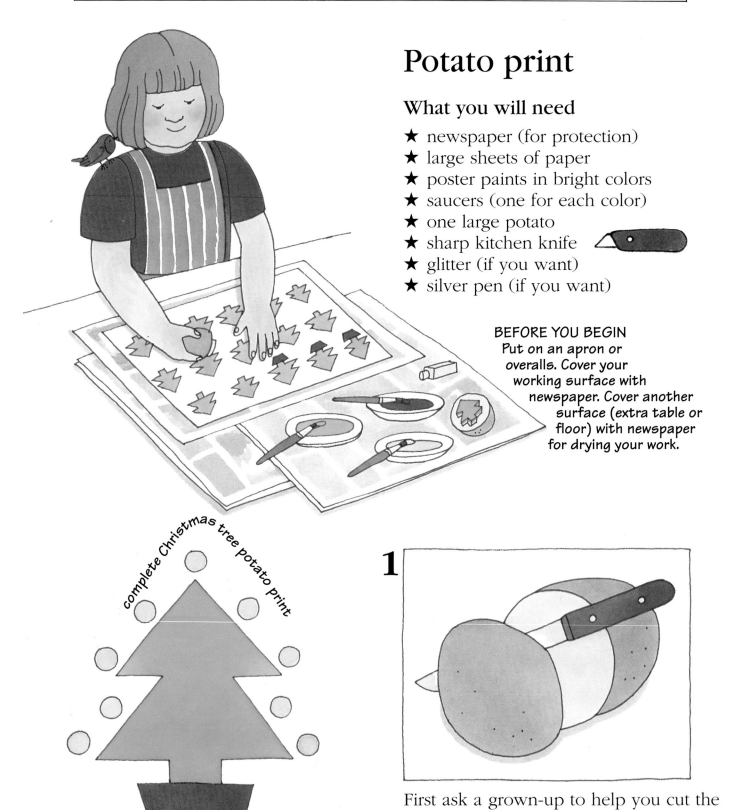

Potato print

What you will need

★ newspaper (for protection)
★ large sheets of paper
★ poster paints in bright colors
★ saucers (one for each color)
★ one large potato
★ sharp kitchen knife
★ glitter (if you want)
★ silver pen (if you want)

BEFORE YOU BEGIN
Put on an apron or
overalls. Cover your
working surface with
newspaper. Cover another
surface (extra table or
floor) with newspaper
for drying your work.

complete Christmas tree potato print

1

First ask a grown-up to help you cut the potato. Cut 2 thick slices.

2

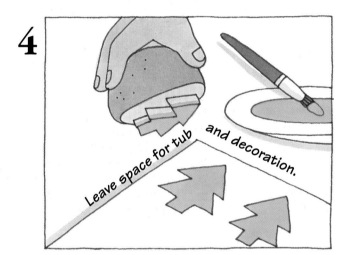

tree

decoration

tub

Cut the simple shapes. Use a
trimming for the decoration.

3

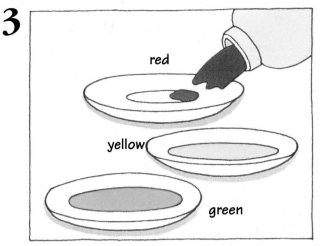

red

yellow

green

Pour a small amount of paint into each
saucer.

4

Leave space for tub and decoration.

Dip the shape into the paint and
print all over the paper.

5

Add the tubs and then the decorations.
Lay the sheet aside to dry.

6

Add glitter to wet paint.

Try these shapes: star, candles, holly.

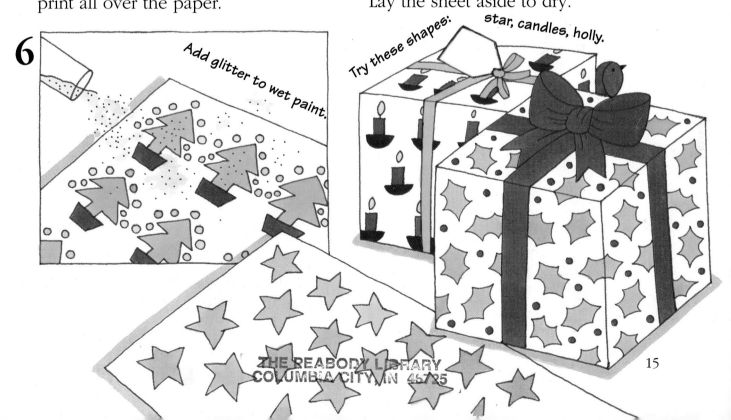

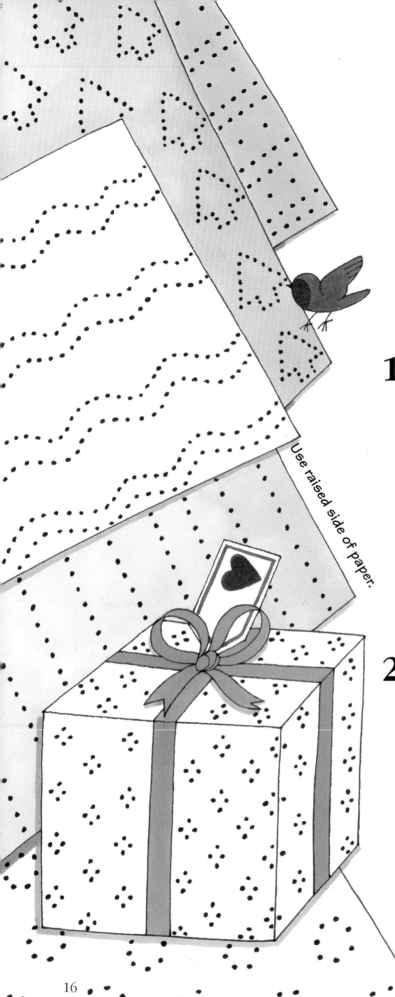

Use raised side of paper.

Pattern of holes

What you will need

★ large sheet of colored paper
★ thin knitting needle or very sharp pencil
★ thick rug or blanket

1

Put the paper on a thick rug or folded blanket. Hold the edges firmly.

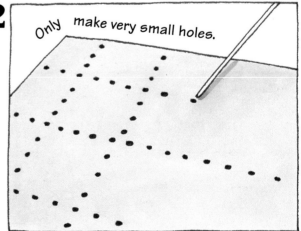

2 Only make very small holes.

Push the knitting needle or sharp pencil through the paper. Try to make a pattern.

Gifts Galore

Each of these presents has a match – except one.
Can you spot the one that has no match?

Desk set

This could be for your teacher or a friend at school, or for someone in your family.

What you will need

★ toilet paper roll tubes (at least 4)
★ scissors
★ old wrapping paper or aluminum foil
★ glue
★ cardboard
★ pencil

1

Cut one very short.

Cut 4 or 5 toilet paper roll tubes to different lengths.

2

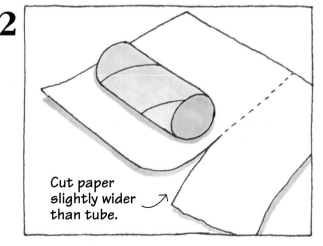

Cut paper slightly wider than tube.

Cut rectangles of old wrapping paper or aluminum foil to cover the tubes.

3

Snip the ends of the paper.

4

Glue down.

Glue the paper to the tubes and tuck the ends in firmly.

5

Put the tubes on a flat surface and glue them together.

6

Take a piece of cardboard and draw around the bottom of the tubes.

7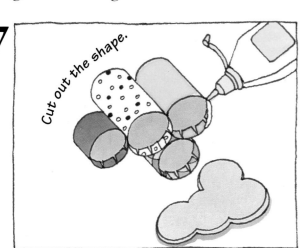

Cut out the shape.

Glue the shaped cardboard to the bottom of the tubes.

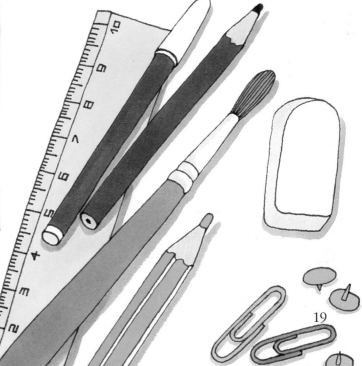

Christmas badges

What you will need

★ cardboard
★ Christmas stencils (if you want)
★ pencil
★ scissors
★ crayons, paints, stickers, glitter, holly
  (for decoration)
★ felt-tip pen (for message)
★ tape
★ double-sided tape
★ safety pin

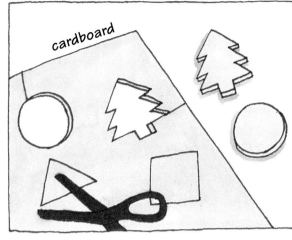

Draw, then cut out the shape of the badge. Use stencils if you want.

Decorate the front of the badge and write a message.

Make a giant badge with a paper plate.

Stick a badge on a card.

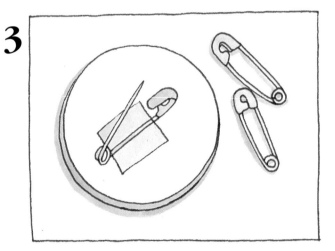

Tape a safety pin to the back of the badge. Close it carefully.

Give these as presents for your teachers or friends.

Chocolate snowballs

What you will need

These quantities make about 15 walnut-sized balls.

★ 3 ½ ounces plain cooking chocolate
★ 5 ounces pitted dates, chopped
★ 3 ½ ounces dried apricots, chopped finely (soak first to moisten)
★ 2 ounces chopped mixed nuts
★ shredded coconut
★ sprinkles
★ hot chocolate or cocoa powder
★ mixing bowl
★ fork
★ small paper muffin cups

BEFORE YOU BEGIN
Wash your hands and put on an apron or overalls. Take out all the things you will need.

1

Use a dish over boiling water.

Ask a grown-up to help you melt the chocolate.

2

Use a fork to mix.

Mash together the melted chocolate, dates, apricots, and nuts.

3

Put in paper muffin cups. *Chill in fridge.*

Form the mixture into little balls. Roll them in the coconut, sprinkles, or chocolate powder.

Christmas present

What you will need

★ large cardboard box
★ scissors or craft knife—be careful!
★ newspaper (for protection)
★ poster paints in bright colors
★ wide foil or paper ribbon
★ tape or stapler
★ stickers, sequins, glitter, tinsel
★ headband
★ piece of white paper or cardboard (for label)
★ felt-tip pen (for message)
★ yarn

BEFORE YOU BEGIN
For painting, put on an apron or overalls and cover a table or the floor with newspaper.
You may need help from a grown-up or friend.

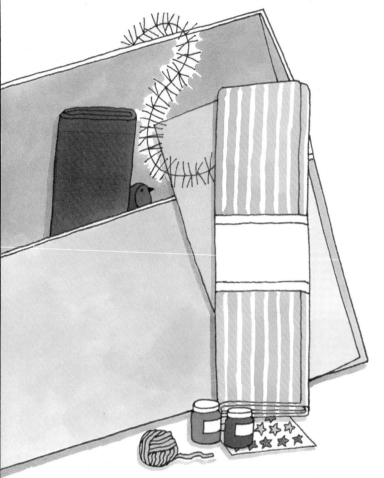

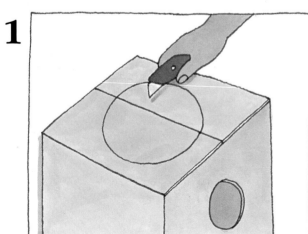

1 Cut a hole in the bottom of a large cardboard box. Cut 2 holes in the sides.

2 Paint the box a bright color.

3

Tape or staple some wide ribbon across the box.

4

Decorate the box with stars, stickers, silver or gold paint, or glitter.

5

Ask someone to help you.

Lower the box carefully over your head. Put your arms through the sides.

6

Make a large ribbon bow. Tape it to a headband.

Tie a label loosely around your wrist.

Wear colored tights to match your package.

Christmas Around the World

Christmas is not only celebrated on December 25. In the Netherlands and Belgium, children expect Santa Claus on the night before St. Nicholas's day, December 6. And on January 6 in Austria, children dress up as the three kings and walk through the snowy streets collecting money and small gifts.

I T A L Y

The **presepio**, the crib or nativity scene, is the most important decoration in Italian homes and churches. In churches, they are often very large, with lights and moving people.

A U S T R A L I A

Christmas in Australia is in the middle of the summer. Families spend the holiday on the beach and eat cold turkey and salad.

D E N M A R K

Children in Denmark have a very special Advent Calendar. It is made of cloth instead of paper and is embroidered with the numbers 1 to 24. Each morning in December children wake up to discover a small present pinned to the right number. Could you make a calendar like this next year?

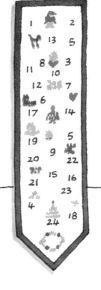

First edition for the United States published 1993 by Barron's Educational Series, Inc.

Text and illustrations © 1991 b small publishing

All inquiries should be addressed to:
Barron's Educational Series, Inc.
250 Wireless Boulevard
Hauppauge, NY 11788

International Standard Book No. 0-8120-1745-5

Design: Lone Morton   Editorial: Catherine Bruzzone
Finished artwork: Naomi Games

Printed in Hong Kong
3456   0987654321

Merry Christmas!

Do you know how to say "Merry Christmas" in Italian, French, German, and Spanish? Which is which? The answers are upside down.

Buon Natale	Frohe Weihnachten—German
Joyeux Noël	Feliz Navidad—Spanish
Feliz Navidad	Joyeux Noël—French
Frohe Weihnachten	Buon Natale—Italian